Loving the Days

The Wesleyan Poetry Program : Volume 93

Loving
the Days

By JOHN WITTE

Wesleyan University Press

MIDDLETOWN, CONNECTICUT

Grateful acknowledgement is made to the following publications, in which some of these poems have appeared: *The American Poetry Review, The Beloit Poetry Journal, Epoch, The Falcon, The Paris Review, Shankpainter, Discover America*, the *San Jose Studies* bicentennial poetry anthology. The poem, "The Crotch Island Quarry" appeared in an earlier version in *The New Yorker*.

The author wishes to thank the Fine Arts Work Center in Provincetown, Massachusetts, for a fellowship in the course of which some of these poems were written.

Library of Congress Cataloging in Publication Data

Witte, John, 1948-
    Loving the days.
    (The Wesleyan poetry program; v. 93)
    I. Title.
PS3573.I917L6   811'.5'4   78-7629
ISBN 0-8195-2093-4
ISBN 0-8195-1093-9 pbk.

Manufactured in the United States of America
First Edition

For Deb

Contents

1

Chasing Hamlet

All night rooting, Hamlet squeezed loose,
a secret pinkness under the wall,
your pet piglet
feeling himself round and free in the city.
Streetlights reddened his tiny eyes.
White clouds hooted from his nostrils.
He sprinted up and down the sweet garbage rows.

You weren't worried. You said
Pigs are among the cleverest creatures we know:
whales descend from pigs.
I imagined Hamlet bobbing on the ocean,
in the sunshine growing huge and thoughtful.
We searched all morning in the park
shattering the frosted shadows of trees.
Now he seems like part of our love getting away.

We found the women hurling their groceries
over their heads, on Main Street, Hamlet
squirting out from under parked cars,
his tail curled tightly behind.
Children shrieked happily.
Policemen toddled on their knees, pleading,
plunking their nightsticks.
A storewindow had broken, blanketing
the sidewalk. A firetruck came
and backed over a streetsign.

Everyone pointed, Hamlet skidding
down Pearl Street by the river.
I don't believe he swam for it,
smoothly cutting through the slushy Kennebec
and across Casco Bay into the open Atlantic.
I think he went to the dump
with its enormous seagulls turning overhead
and waited for the town dogs.

How It Ended

Still asleep, she stepped out
naked over the lake, touching with her feet
the pitted granite landing.
She dove.
The wrinkles smoothed
she was under so long.
Fingerlings nibbled at the shore.

Saxtons River flooded the week
we were away, rolling cars
over the South Londonderry waterfall.
My neighbor came over the radio asking
for his calf back. He'd give fifty dollars.

Driving the hours home, detoured,
the aspens doubled over,
pointing to the sea. She was my
last lover steering.
From his yard where a man gathered
ruined belongings a cat
darted under our front wheels.

She stopped the car.
Minnows flashed in the ditchwater.
She gasped like a child
for each passing thing.

The Nighthawk

Called Goatsucker
for his habit, secret bird,
sweet nanny milk warm on his throat.
He pumped his wings. Drank.
For this the goatherd drove him
back into the shrill sky.

Thought bird, aerialist,
called Nightjar now,
swooping evolutions,
craw cram-full of smashed insects.

By twilight the nighthawk cry
is a long nail, a root
ripped from its hole in the air.
Since you left he lets the daylight slide
opalescent into the river,
saves nothing,
builds no nest.

The moon is loosened.
This is how the evening comes apart.

Terrified at the Family Reunion
in Mendota, Illinois

What did I know, skinny kid
flown from the suburbs?

Today I dreamed out
the brittle voices, tobacco spit
through teeth under the clutch of oaks.
The air squeezed us.
A distant relation, uncle
blank as a barn and full
or not of his own reasons: balancing
his beer he swatted me

from his sight. Dazed
over the peafield,
a tiny heart tapping in my left cheek,

in my dream what happens
is a warm rain
begins. His brown palm
glides toward me like a bird.
Grandpa's plowshares are streaming rust.
Arrowheads click past.

Everything is becoming less
and less possible.

Wild Bill at Troy Grove, Ill.

I aim your ivory-handled revolver at the sofa
but don't shoot. The old woman
enters with a teapot.
You were always Jim Hickok here,
a quiet boy helping with the hay. If you weren't
at home maybe you were fishing, who knows.
Who could believe the stories?
Were you shown a sign: a catfish
big as a man slumbering on the bottom?
Why did they call you Bill?

From the 1870 portrait it's clear
we're related, this woman and I
have your sharp bones in our faces, you cutting
loose at 18 thinking Christ I have shot a man
through the heart I had to. You made yourself
a cop: everyone had to behave.
Bored, you went to work for Custer and died
in Dodge. False. They ambushed the wrong man.
You write to the newspaper about this
and ride through town with your hair long.
Women look up startled.
Indians spring from the bushes. You keep shooting
coins out of the sky and glaring into our eyes.

In the window I can see nothing
but rows of corn, the black Interstate
snaking west. The six-gun
is on the table,
a shrieking eagle raised on the grip.
The woman is pouring tea, she is talking.

Halfway to Oregon

West of Seward cicadas shout.
Pigs whale through muck
and moon up
at the Interstate. Farms spatter
the windshield: cabbage leaf,
horseblood. Nebraska
like a loss of will lies down.

The radio is unclear. Already
the Lincoln station sinks back
in the skywaves. Twisting
the dial I pick up
thunderheads jabbing lightning.

If we could see coming what is
coming nothing would budge us.
We'd cut the engine
and tap a rootbeer bottle
on the steering wheel forever.

I would have married Maine.
A dozen times since Chicago
I have driven on myself
rolled and burned.
Not the Pacific.
Not all the miles high
mares' tails and blue Cascades. Not Oregon.

From the Car to Corvallis, Oregon

Evening smoke suffers up the valley
touching the stooped shells of cars
abandoned. Here someone tried
everything he knew,
the seats rising wet and sexual,
fenders flying off
like heavy birds.

This is the season to burn back
wheat and rye
and wring clouds from the fields.

Idling pickups on the shoulder lovers
slide tongues over teeth
and smile: the field leaps,
bristling stars and signs.

I remember Great Pond full of stars,
in Maine, and how we trembled after.
These were things I had not known.
How a woman could push
her face down
hot with tears into her hands.
Or how I could leave anyway
and hide myself on the road.

To a Friend in Vermont

My neighbors are letting loose
red and yellow hair
from their fireplaces, maple and birch
woodsmoke. The glutted river
rolls in bed.

Your belly hardened when I
weaseled under the sweater,
then relaxed: your breasts
slipped over my cheeks,
Emily, you'd pushed through snow
clear from town to mind the woodstove.
I tasted the warm sugar maple
smoke on your face.

The chainsaw ticked while it cooled
in the hall. New snow
wheeled off Glebe Mountain.

A dog somewhere opens his throat
and barks. He's getting ready,
hefting his voice. Emily, it rains here
ten days at a time.

A cat leaps into the road.
Tons of water swerve under the city.

Oregon Juncos

The female took off
dirt-colored through the branches
ringing the china bell in her throat.
They have two voices, you said.
I pushed my face into your hair.

Gliding down green streets
through the cedar she sounds this morning
lovelier than ever.
She might be pregnant already,
speckled moons drifting toward her
in the crush of jays: she has flown
a thousand miles for this,
for every blue jay to notice
when her wing lifts, her staggering
white underparts. The snap
of her bloodbrown iris. Her mate at a distance
pumping his whole body, yelling Where
are you Where
are you. Her bell
keeps shifting in the morning air.

April Morning

I have returned at night to your door
for the last time. I kneel in the mud
by the river and turn up a rotted log.

Insects clambering over each others' eggs
convey their dead in their mouths
down tunnels. Some gather
small apples back into darkness.
I replace the log on its cold impression.

I'm not alone. Beside me is the pigtailed
woman I walked here with
slowly over cinders and rusted rails
into the thick rivergrass.
Killdeer burst out wildly
crying us away from new nests. She is telling me
her friend's baby is a connoisseur of dirt.
A heron lifts, blue
wings aching over the water. I stagger
into her, pointing to the madhouse
of birds overhead.

Whatever you thought you could make happen to
me by treating me the way you did you were wrong.

My brain is filled with blood.
Birds. The world

is filled with women.

To Her Last Lover

I'm cracking the cat's fleas: a little blood
sucked under the body hairs. Mostly
they get away. I'm not so quick
as she is with her smile, her hand
crouched in the thicket of nerves. You thought
you'd had enough of her and her cat's fleas, her
thighs, her soft snore.

You still make her laugh when you call:
she comes and leans absently against me.
When your father finally died
in his sleep she knew about it: she dreamed
of the slow crab that dragged him under.
Take the next plane, you begged,
and help me rake the leaves.
She cried and said nothing.

I met you once. You were lying down
with your foot bandaged, gored by a nail.

Jim, you treated her badly,
and she hasn't forgotten.
I have treated women badly.
I have an old kind father. I can't explain it,
the ground is so often brittle with leaves.

We're all trying to move forward.
Please do not call here any more.
Come and take your guitar and go.

Leaving You in Oregon

Deborah that's a common name, drab hay
damp in the morning, meadow mice
jumping the stubble for cover.
What happened
under your belly is still hard
to explain: lips into vulva, supple
birds stroking wind and lifting. Even packing
up and leaving this part of the world
drenched, houses swollen in fog,
I keep finding you, here, at home
on a flowering shrub, there swung along
birdheavy telephone wires. When I cast off

east across the continent, discovering
America in reverse, the asphalt Indies,
you'll be there first, oilslick
Pocahontas, the playful one.
Over kelptangled piers, codfish
broken on the road, you'll loft my traveling
bag into the sky like helium. You
woman holding the earth together, you make me
try to make sense.

Today before it rained the cottonwoods let down
white braids, the air heavy
as floodwater shook purple
lupine and trillium in the current.
Light flipping like fish in the trees,
(the words finally coming to me),
rain and sun falling together,
commonplaces,
the everyday facts return.

Fathers

Bees crash in blistered clover
hurt. You can see this: they snuggle to root, hive,
stabbing the air behind. You touch slowly
with your tongue the bony folds of your palate,
the fleshy part farther back: *uvula,* grape.
You take yourself inside.

Swinging almond arms your woman
murmurs in the sun room. Sofa.
Urging the rocker. Now at the window: nothing
feels right. At last she stands
naked on the oak floor.

Your first love let you touch her nipples.
You remembered purple, parachuting
down, clung to umbilical, the lucent amnion
unfurling after. She said Wait. I hardly know you.
You hardly knew yourself.

Her father stank of tar. Ashes. Gas.
Slumped working a sliver from his palm.
She looked at her hands. Papa.
She awoke hearing the night freight
bumping cargo over the ties.

Later you realized your lovers, thumping
the small of your back like wings.
They cried. They couldn't say why
their fathers carried their arms at such odd angles,
executives home late bruised around the eyes.
Everything in the room was plugged in.

Today your woman is calling her father
by his first name: he doesn't appear. An astronaut.
She can't recall. A spy. Assassin. The verdict
returned, they strapped him in a flying chair
and sent him off. Outside
rain pocks dropped leaves, colored
mittens.

After the Abortion

I have never seen you so simply
asleep, hugging your knees,
all your small bones gathered in.

Our neighbor appears in the window,
an old woman sweeping the sidewalk,
skitch skitch skitch, sweeping the drive,
the street, she's bent to her task: to sweep
off the world.

During the surgery I heard screams,
I thought, faintly through the wall.
What could I do but sit. Stare
at the door. Keep staring. Part of me
aborted, too: a scrap
tore loose.
I imagined a road map
crumpled, blue and red stains.
I was so glad to see you I could hardly
walk, either.

She's sunk in a kind of clarity,
that old woman: she will have the world clean.
She's lost enough. She pulls with her broom
at the pebbles in the cracks.

She'll never finish her work now:
more red leaves are falling.

Letter from Land's End

Winter is here. The richest men have left
without a word: Hughes, Onassis and Getty
rising over the frozen earth.
I've just arrived.

The Pilgrims landed in 1620. In my dream
I see you smiling with your legs
around a new lover and grind
my teeth awake. The sky
naked of angels, I stoop down
for a shell, feather, a smoothed
pebble: roll it slowly between my fingers.

This is your nipple. Your pear tree

shivering wildly in the backyard,
I remember: you were in there shaking,
grasping the tree limbs with your own.
Pears dropped into the long grass.
Moths darted up.

I have put America between us
for reasons of money. This will be
the coldest winter of all.
Lowell has left the world in a taxi.

2

Dreaming the Oregon Trail

Mother-of-pearl fires from the parapets
and walls gem light down
on the river, from farm
to farm. Opal
inset mosaic like Dr. Gatling's
gun scatters the last light.
From this elevation, through a cleft
in the ridge it might have been
conifers only: it was the Holy City.
We had dust enough on our faces.

Beholding the valley a woman
declares *Minneapolis*. I remember
my instructions, the crushed leaf
of paper sweated through: *Take all
the seeds and little trees
and place them on the ground — everything
will appear maidenly.*

An old man is crying *Salzburg,
Salzburg!* others, *Cincinnati! Buffalo!*
pronouncing the names of places
where they were born, where they knew
a woman, where they were promised.

Since Snake River
I have watched the backbone curve
under the shift of a girl named Eliza.
A tiny bell, a wren
precedes us down the slope.

Weeding the Beanfield

Swallows are plucking
startled insects out of the air.
Women's laughter, the click
of washed plate, jangling silverware,
dinner is a kind of victory.
We talk football, old enough to know how
shouts echo under the helmet,
but not enough to fight in Asia.
We're kids. Any moment
we might make a run for it.

With Leo, who disappeared
in the heat of June
under the community carp pond,
I'm bending through the cool Illinois evening,
dragging up nets of morning glory,
bluemouthed flowers
from the clinging beans.

My neighbor won't empty her mailbox.
The boy is all right, she says, her last G.I.
flown into the jungle — she won't
hear about it. She rehearses
the recipe for spaghetti.

In this light, eight years arriving,
the field could be calm water,
the tiny bean blossoms
stars.

From Memory

He broke his back for the U.S. Army.
They tapped into his spine
a thin wedge of shinbone,
pegged and bolted his back up
straight as furniture. So you think
of him, Lester: seated in a greatcoat.
You have a son's memory.

Over and over you
dreamed the tractor bursting
driverless through the barn door.
The boulders in the wall all day
pushed one another. Your mother held back
her tears, the bedpost nicked
from butternuts he'd slapped open
and shared under the warm quilt.

His face stretched in the wind
when he tried to stand,

a son remembers
his father's face: pink as radish,
becoming clear and etched
like crystal. Transparent,
you sense him reaching for the shotgun,

reappearing, some hours later
in the backyard,
crashing out of the appletree.

The Bear that Alec Killed

Finally Alec Kennedy has killed the bear
that killed his cow, pounding a 30.30 slug
like a stake through that malevolent heart,
and he is satisfied. On the front page
of the Machias Valley News Observer
the bear's great eyes shine back,
mooning in the flash,
those cow-devouring eyes.

I would be the last to tell him
that he has bombed the moonlight
out of the women and children
of the city of this animal's heart.
Or that come spring
a bear will pop up in his pasture.

Here in Jacksonville, Maine
it's hardly noticed: one bear less,
an old tired and hungry male
scavenging for chickenscraps;
one shot, one cry at dusk,
a groan in the interminable mumble
backstage of a nation's dream.
Alec himself will fall as quietly.

The Newark Rebellion
July, 1967

All day the road. At night the moon
sleeks the road, fluting down gutters.
I am waiting in a rented room to sink asleep.
Silverfish slid from dry bookbindings
ease across ceiling and walls.

I fingerfuck her three four times,
my old lady, really get her gushing
before I put it to her. Tony
unlocks the filling station,
starts the sign revolving—
Here we are, it says, Here.
Already the sun bangs off the asphalt.

Birdboned children plunge
alleys. On the back wall,
between rest rooms they rough out vaginas
in green, Day-Glo penises: Fuck Pig.
Waiting for customers I hear them stagger
in the splintered glass.

Man, give us some gas,
a collapsed Lincoln idling,
little gas for my lawnmower.
I am nearly a brother: I have eaten
peanut butter from this same jar.
Got me a big lawn
fulla grass out in the suburbs.
Like a brother he considers killing me.

Sirens all night climb ramshackle
tenements, curbstones heaved
shimmering through plate.
Flames, plundered televisions: people
literally shopping in there.
The whole town is gone,
explained Mayor Addonizio.
A woman with a broom handle
punches in precinct windows.

I can't give you gas
in an open container.
There's a law. He says nothing and we wait
over thousands of gallons of high test.

After ten years
I am floating up under a bedsheet
here on the West Coast.
If I knock on the wall and shout
come in
the room fills with glittering police.

Power Failure

In darkness someone returns
his glass to the table with a soft tick.
We question the roof.
A huge oak has not toppled
over the wires. We reach out
our hands at the ends of our arms.

Flames appear gliding up the stairs.
Lovers rise and paddle
through the air over Pennsylvania.
The farmer drifts over his fields, in moonlight
admiring the pattern: alfalfa, drainage, sweet corn.
Now the police are playing their sirens.

Night surges over the buildings,
against the picture window with a few stars.

The city has vanished.
The children have shut their eyes.
How will we find our way back.

The New Clerk

The last person to hold his job
was robbed and shot. Fluorescent
soup cans throb on the shelf. A few customers
curve their shoulders forward in bewilderment.
His boss said Lightning never strikes twice.

Once he saw a pellet of light, a high pop
fly arc past black clouds. The outfielder
waiting to make the catch raised his glove
but a long spark attached to him.
Everyone laughed you couldn't
help it: a kid jumping at the end of a bright string.
He lived. He forgot
everything: he had to start again.

The store is rounded to a globe
in the fisheye mirror,
broccoli, hammers, light bulbs: a dwarf
planet rolling through the darkness.
The girl in a flowered blouse reading a comic,
the man buying beer — the sharp chill on his palm:
a world with a killer in it.

How did this happen.

A man approaches holding
a jar of cinnamon.

Poem for the New Year

The radio yammers news: my country
bullying the world into mud huts, I've
toppled the salt.
Grains skitter
the table and stop. Landlocked
kings kept sea salt
humping overland donkeyback, fine silk
slipping on the nipples of the merchant's girl.
Trails are worn by animals seeking
salt it is essential.

Today my sister's son named for me
braided his fingers through mine
from museum to wharf. Freighters
dragged gigantic chains.
On the subway steps scuffed hollow
as riverbottom he cried Stars, stars!
And hard sparks were gleaming in the granite.

For luck we toss spilled salt into the air
over our left shoulder. Like this. Tonight
another orbit of the planet begins.

Snow gusts onto the window.
On his bedroom wall the boy taps to me.
He taps. Listens. He taps.
Hello, I knock back: Here I am.
Snowflakes stream down the glass.

Wendy, after Eight Years

The war is over. A fire is piled
with the small garments of the enemy.
They say at last the war is over.

Which war.

Tonight I am shiftless as a fat raccoon
come to lie in the woods by the lake
and listen. Bats,
tiny faces are loose in the air
but their voices can't be heard.

Your mother once told me
you were born covered with fur. Daughter
of my friends' broken marriage, I remember you
lissome in the meadow, with semi-circular
shadows under your breasts. Love becomes
with time and talk less possible.

Your father has married again somewhere.
The creek behind your house keeps pulling
stones apart into smaller stones.

We were all hoping for better than this.
You must be a woman now, I can't imagine.

Catfish Reunion

With three or four lines out,
fishing for food,
the big black men hunched in the reeds.
We fished for adventure,
getting dirty after gradeschool.

They said *We come from blue Newark*
where the river's all
factory acid.

Today
when I think of catfish
I'll forget where I am
and slip out over the long cloudy bottoms
to follow them.
All the silent fishermen are there.
Together we thread past
jangling hooks and lures.

Soon we'll be choked back
to the headwaters
where there's nothing left
but to climb up into the rain.

3
Loving the Days

The Man Who Loved Sunday

I can't complain. The sun is coming
down on each roof alike, a beacon
to steer the cars home. I like my car.
Look. My neighbor tugging his poodle.
You can't sniff every hydrant: he's right.
You can't kiss all the pretty girls. My wife
smiles at the mashed potatoes. Like clouds,
she says, you ever think of that? What
are we supposed to think?
This is how things are.
Television shines in the living room.
I could watch the actors all night,
they're so thin and jumpy.
I don't mind.
You have to kneel down somewhere.

The Man Who Loved Monday

Night long into my walk I can't see where
my feet land. I feel
twigs snap through my shoes, damp
stalks buckle their spines.
I stub the curb.
The trees whistle with birds nervously
folding and unfolding their wings.
I'm not frightened. I feel
mud underfoot, puffy water, the air thickened
with creatures: The Pecking Hen, The Woman
with Shopping Bags, an impossible look in her eye.
Stars bob and wallow. I lift into the moonlight
my hand pink as a baby's!

Did I invite you to read this?
I keep to myself.

The Man Who Loved Tuesday

The streets are full of kooks: don't tell me.
Someone is waiting to jump you. If you don't
learn to use your hands you won't have a prayer.
The man beside you. What is he thinking?
Me, I go to the gym. Even asleep I practice
moves: my enemy has me
in holds I've never seen, for hours
deadlocked. His slippery limbs smell
like fish, he keeps changing shape. It's hard
work: no one ever said it wouldn't be.
Here are the maggots on your lips.
Any moment
you might lose
control yourself and
grab someone by the hair.

The Man Who Loved Wednesday

Pawn to King four. Your move. 'Dig in,'
I tell the children. I make them play
chess: teaches them who gets pushed in the shit.
They'll be whipping their old man one day.
I learned it hawking News at the corner,
the snot still on my face.
I began to scrap.
And here I am. The Knight you're lifting is carved
ivory. Weigh it on your palm. You can see why I hate
paying those jerk-offs welfare: 'Help your own.'
There was no one left for me
to help. At night I hear my sister
in the room, her gums bleeding.

My walls are heavy with art. You have to be
hungry for it. Your move.

The Man Who Loved Thursday

Listen to that wind — bullets clattering the maple.
Parked cars rock on their springs.
A bucket leaves its orbit and wobbles around
the yard, surprised, becoming something else.
A street sign wags. Jefferson said what?
The tree of liberty must be refreshed from time
to time? I want it now, tonight: I'm ready.
In eight minutes the Capitol dome will crack,
an enormous wing appearing through the roof.
All state employees will be awakened and machine-gunned,
all documents shredded, pigs sliced and plowed under.
I will hammer my father into the ground. There will be
more room inside than I can remember ever.
The lightning has struck.
Here comes the thunder.

The Man Who Loved Friday

Misery, says the housefly.
Lifting an apple from the bowl
I grip the stem and twist and say
She loves me. And twisting again She loves
me not, I don't care: I'll never forget
her thighs swooped to her belly. I slide
my tongue over the apple, and twist.
She loves me: the stem pops,
thumping the seeds at the core.

Snow has drifted all afternoon into the city,
gathering over the sharp gravel on the parking lot.
Do I ask for so much?
I'd reach for her asleep
across the continent, the world a moment
small enough to grasp and warm.

The Man Who Loved Saturday

Nothing was here when I came: oceans
wore out the earth. Days passed outlandishly
named. Nothing happened. A shorebird landed
nimbly printing its feet in wet sand.
Nothing happened and nothing happened and then
the manufacturers beached their oily barges.

You have to make a start.
There are seven ways through the week
and a few good nouns: star, blood, apple.
It isn't much. It isn't anything
gold beaten into fragile figurines, only

clear. I made this for you.
I love you. I can't help myself. I'm loving
every minute of it. I won't comb my hair.
I'll leave the house in a crazy hat.

4

Uncle Steph

Birch —
nervous trees leaning over a river:
I reach for food in the dark
cupboard you cut
and rubbed from birch.
Today you lifted the hammer and fell
silently through your weak heart.
Ringing on the concrete
all the nails spilled from your pouch.

All the sparrows in Mendota rose
flinging lice in the summer air.
Carpenters struck their thumbs,
cursed, and went on hammering.
All the boards in the house
built to last
rushed into the soil
and out again in thin green leaves,

pale trees rising, a distant nephew
the whole day listening, unsure.

The Church at the Corner
of Winter and Elm

Watch it.
Turning this corner might land you plump
sheepish in the teeth
of someone's wedding, or underfoot
his funeral procession,
a stranger.

You must resist the desire to disappear.
Impersonate
the rebel son slunk back from Amsterdam
to watch the coffin hole plugged.
See if they don't touch your elbow,
commiserate: every family has one.
In organ thunder
people are ready for anything,
a mysterious lover
lean as a pickerel slipping
through bridesmaids' willowy arms.

Today it's another man's undertaking.
You'll get your chance shortly.

In the meantime, listen:
someone hauls down the bellcord,
then gives it back
into the steeple.
The bell metal rings spread
exactly as calm water
grazed by a swallow.
Again he pulls the cord.

Mowing a Roadside
in Woodbury, Connecticut

Drunk slightly and tired with the guests
I lurched in the dark by the lake.
Stumbling, stabbed fast in blackberry
thorns, I said now, you treefrogs,
give me back my first house
in the violets. I am composed
of peepers and rubbing crickets.

I did not become a bird
and hurl myself homing on the sky.
I did not become a hound
sniffing the thin trail of myself.
I stepped forward,
alive in a cloud of biting flies.

This morning I am lackadaisical
in wildflowers, swiping the bright
scythe under purple lupine and pigweed.
Indian paintbrush shimmers red
as broken coals.
Honeybees spin at my waist.
Pickerel bolt under the water lilies.

A tohee is singing herself awake.
She has her secrets.
I have mine.
We are not moving to a master.

Happy the Walker

The apples. Today the apples
are cunning. The sun bubbles
from the ocean, each stone quick
pulling in its legs.
The waves keep milling clamshells
and pitching up the whorled
chambered ones with voices.

I have all morning
ransacked my brain for that
slithery woodchuck, the whiskered
xylophone in his mouth,
scuffling home fat,
full of songbirds:
I'd have seized him but you came.

Now everyone is hungry.
The heart the little bag of blood
is sad and hungry.
How we'd love to leave the children run
and go ourselves alone down the beach.
Never come back.
Come back drunk.
You name it.
We've driven far enough
all these cars down the only road.

I'd catch a rabbit
in my hand I am that patient.
I'd sit on a stone
before the moving
elbows of the sea and eat.

Perely Nicholson's Delight

Copper-bottomed pots golden on the north wall,
from the kitchen he watched the pasture
aspens passing fire up Hawks Ridge.
Dawn.
Today he'd butcher the yearling Hereford,

a man's face
shining on the sledge hammer.

Stemming chokecherries
into a tin bowl between her knees
his old woman hears voices now, voices,
the whole crowd of people most dear to her.
She warbles softly all day.
She startles.
When the skull explodes she might
pitch the red berries over the grass.

He'll speak to the dogs, let them
down on the glistening viscera. Spatter.
Flourish pale sacs clear to town.

The calf seems naked,
following him with her eyes.

My Neighbor Hosing Her Lawn
in the Dark

And now the roses — arcing cool rain
into the garden, the dry loam talks almost.
Heavy blossoms rock on their stems.
All afternoon bending her rake, white oak
leaves catching on her
dizzy head, she rolled brittle piles into the fire.

Where is her husband?
From her stoop she can reach the whole lawn,
swishing spray over the grass.
What did their impossible son shout at him?
Doors slammed, cups springing from their saucers.
Now the tomatoes. Now
the sunflowers looking down.
Their only child, what with the war
and the payments, and then he was gone.

She is dreaming on the dark porch,
water rumbling in the hose.
Flowers grow lush
grasping her hem and hand — and now
the roses, now vegetables sprawled on the soil.
Her beauty is still inside,
in a summer dress wandering
back and forth through the weedy field.

Three Windows

Words appear in the mist
behind a window, someone looming in red,
tracing letters with his finger. I can see him
blurred through his writing, his message
private, backwards.

From her bedroom a woman waves to me. I thought
she waved to me: she
cleans her window only,
with a white rag
stroking the glass side to side.

A man is making ridiculous faces
from his window over the calm harbor.
I realize he is singing.
Leaving a trail in the sand
a boy pulls a blue rowboat by a rope,
and presses it into the water.

Louise's Motel

She wants to clean your room.
She knocks and listens,
a flurry of dirty linen
like milkweed broken from her side.
Passing trucks drum the glass: she wonders
did you sleep soundly, tall and quiet as her own
boy, did you dream of snow falling on the Interstate?
Did she hear your dog cough?
But you've gone. Opening
her son's door like this, a bomb
might have gone off, so scattered
everything was years back. She doesn't hear
the dog behind her, claws ticking concrete.

He holds the booklet *Rabies* closed in his lap.
They wheeled his wife into the white emergency
room. He shoots the dog in his mind,
black fur rolling forward in the dry ditch. He
shoots the dog in his mind. He roams
in the fog behind his cataracts, hunting.
He hates the dog for getting away.
He hates to stumble into customers
by the ice machine. The drunks colliding, why
are they here, the one night lovers
leaving in separate cars.
Where is my son?
"The rabid dog may swallow
pieces of wood, coal, metal or carpet."

The motel is vacant.
Midges trip on the pool surface.
Through her body on the white table Louise
pumps the dog's venom. In her
dream she sees each room blazing,

orange flames swirling behind the picture windows. The
boy is in the office trying to speak, maybe a bone is cross-
ways in his throat. The black dog watches him. A tiny scar
beneath his eyebrow, he turns striding back to his car.
Wait,

I'm shouting Wait, running after you, my hair coming
loose my clothes each fiber unraveling, Don't Go We've
Kept Your Room The Way It Was, my shoes peeling away,
your father running too: look at him lurching on the hot
asphalt, naked, sagging onto the highway, the car getting
smaller, we're

laughing, holding hands under the birches on the dirt
road that entirely encircles the lake. I can smell the mush-
rooms. I'm carrying the basket where we put the mush-
rooms. The black dog runs ahead and waits for us excitedly.
Again he runs ahead.

Dream of Returning to Earth

Lush, she squeezes her vagina over.
How do you feel.

The bed lifts off the floor. Books open
and flap through the room.
Can you hear me?
In the window a blue planet,
the earth is turning its jewelry.

The spacecraft is responding well,
my health is good, the stars are very bright.
My arms rise when I sleep and hang
overhead like a small child's
wanting a lift. I have failed
to observe the gods: there are no
honeybees here, or flutes. No air. Fire
a gun nothing is heard.
The bullet travels forever.

The children are asking for me. I am dizzy
on the swing my stomach sinks and
I stop weightless at the top.
Girls squeal in the wind
pressing their dresses down.

I drop back covered with flames,
a human heart in a falling star.

I've landed behind a railroad embankment.
Grasshoppers are shrieking.
A car skids forward — a woman leaps
out, blood pulsing from her forehead.
I have to shout to be heard:
Please direct me to a telephone!

To My Sister Lois

Small airplanes moan in the fog
like departed souls. They circle
once over the town and ascend blinking.

The photograph arrived today: your baby
dropped out of the sky, stunned
in his crib, peering dizzily up.
I think he's about to smile.

No one can lift him, heavy
as an automobile his father cannot,
as a sack of gold his grandfather cannot, he's ugly
as a mudpuppy to his childless aunt, but
weightless to you
toward whose nipples he drifts.

What can I tell you about myself.
Everything you predicted has occurred: I keep
too much alone. Harvesting the fog
the stars are sharpened.
The plum trees have begun to bloom
white. I won't be coming home.

Your son waggles his feet at the camera.
Even inside you his soles grew thick.
Soon he'll stand. Fall.
You can lace him into the heaviest shoes on earth,
he'll stagger away.

Winter Apples

for Samuel Ogden

Sam you have the last apples left
in Vermont, in an oak barrel,
fragrant as embers. You watch
the orchard blacken in the hatchet wind.
Neighbor or not, you'll get a good price.

Old Yankee there you go out the back window
fiddling over the rigid garden. Bach's Fugue
in C Minor and all the Sunday chamber group's
dragged underground. The viola following
his carcinoma under like a stone. The cellist
clasping a root, they play their parts back
from a room in the earth. You who never dropped
an apple still cannot take your life:
someone always appears at the nick
of time.

This is not what you waited so long for,
your children falling through the city.
Mamie in white thought to be in a gentle sleep.
The County will broaden the road through the village.
The river grips its garbage. At least
they'll never make a museum out of the snow-
drifted Nelson farm, the old Landgrove Inn
where there was no battle, no blood
plashing the floorboards, just
tuckered patriots sheltering their stew,
listening to the wind in the chimney,
thinking only of home.

Stop fighting, Sam.
We're as firmly held to this land
as we'll ever be. The apples have kept
sharp and bright against the roof of my mouth.
We've won.

The Crotch Island Quarry, Maine

Deer Isle Pink, for seventy years, like roses
floated across Jericho Bay,
gaining Stonington — granite
block stacked and numbered
on an oily barge.

Quick shrills on the Company whistle meant
Accident and the children watched for
the boat with the broken.
A stone cut loose spun
Mary Prescott's father into the quarry pit.
You could feel the crack: it went
almost around his head.
All he could taste was peas.

New York City starved for granite —
in 1902, one hundred twenty-one thousand tons
for Manhattan's Ninth Regiment Armory alone —
and the orders lined up:
Williamsburg and East River Bridges, Fine Arts
Museum in Boston, the Security Building
in Los Angeles. Ida Mae Eaton's boarding-house
angels wrestled quarrymen,
and dandies at the wedding-cake
Stonington Hotel Virginia-reeled the ladies.
The Cathedral of St. John the Divine
waited for word.

Herman Walker's wife snipped off his socks
to pillow the thin of his wrists.
Apprenticed, he lit the charge
and ran. They sent him back
crabwise when the powder didn't catch.
Nothing held together.

The stonecutters ground
to forty tons the fountain bowl
for the Rockefellers' Tarrytown estate.
They sank
into the gardens of their lungs,
silicosis blossom and bud.

Fifteen hundred stones
rose into the light
for Kennedy's memorial at Arlington,
1966, and the quarry froze shut.
Come spring, there were snakes on the island.

The old quarrymen remember best
their round dinner pails, how their women
treated them on the job.
At the bottom was a well for tea,
over that a section for soup,
then a place for sandwiches,
and on top room for a large pie.
Set the pail over a fire
and the tea warmed your whole meal.

Boston is pinned by silver
slivers of glass and steel. No one calls
for granite. Over the island,
deep in timothy and bay bush, the quarry
rails meander to the wharf.
The stones appear fleshy.
Feldspars, the sorrel flecks
they call "horses in the granite"
catch your eye. Kennedy's memorial
has them. A summer rainstorm and the stone
is skittish with horses.